Martin R. Phillips

NORSE

MYTHOLOGY

Hill Tech Ventures Inc.
Publishing Division | Nanaimo, Canada
Printed in the United States

NORSE

MYTHOLOGY

Discover the Ancient Secrets of

Norse Mythology

MARTIN R. PHILLIPS

ABOUT THE AUTHOR

MARTIN R. PHILLIPS

Martin R. Phillips is an extremely passionate historian, archaeologist, and most recently a writer. Ever since Martin was a young boy he has been fascinated with ancient cultures and civilizations.

In 1990, Martin graduated with distinction from the University of Cambridge with a double major in History and Archaeology. Upon graduation, Martin worked as an archeologist and travelled the world working in various excavation sites. Over the years, while working as an archaeologist, Martin became very well cultured and gained great insights into some of the most historic civilizations to ever exist. This first hand insight into the ancient cultures of the world is what sparked Martin's newest passion, history writing and story telling.

In 2012, Martin decided to retire from archeology to focus on writing. Over the years he has seen and experienced a great deal of fascinating things from all over world. Martin now spends the majority of his free time putting all of his research, experience, and thoughts onto paper in an attempt to share his knowledge of the ancient cultures with the world.

Over the past few years Martin has excelled in his writings. His narrative style has a way of combining the cold hard facts with a story teller's intrigue which makes for an excellent reading experience.

"Live your life to the fullest and enjoy the journey!"

- Martin R. Phillips

TABLE OF CONTENTS

INTRODUCTION

The religion of the Norse or, as they referred to it, Tradition, has captured the minds of many. Though the religion and beliefs of the Vikings are largely out of practice in the world today, the influence of this religion lives on, and in a very profound way.

In the modern day, we see Norse mythos cropping up in movies, television and anime, as well as video games such as Final Fantasy VII, and in comic books. This interest has also reached into the world of music, both from indigenous genres such as the black metal of Norway and other Scandinavian countries, but can be found in various other forms of music and artistic expression.

But what *did* the Norse believe? How did they view the world and what was their conception of their gods? In this book, it is my aim to give you, the reader, an overview of Norse mythology in a way that's not only informative, but interesting.

As with my other texts on mythology (Greek Mythology and Egyptian Mythology) I've found the most effective way to communicate the stories and religion of the Norse is through their stories.

Like many societies, much of Norse lore has been lost to the ages. However, there are a few good sources in this regard, specifically the Eddas. The Poetic Edda in particular is a treasure-trove of insight into the Norse belief system and, through that lens, the Norse way of life.

One thing worthy of mention here is that the central texts still extant on Norse Tradition, namely, the Poetic Edda and the Prose Edda, were written in the thirteenth century. The Tradition, however, was around long before that. As this is the case, much of the knowledge that we now have of the Norse is incomplete and, in some cases, the Poetic Edda disagrees with the Prose Edda. The Poetic Edda, as mentioned above, is particularly insightful, however, as it collects and shares many of the stories of the Norse people.

While this book is not a complete record of the Norse beliefs (and such a record is, to my knowledge, nonexistent,) it has been my pleasure to assemble some of the most pertinent and interesting myths of the Norse. We'll find Odin on his many quests for knowledge and wisdom, the formation of the world out of the body of a giant and we even find Thor in a veiled wedding dress (no, seriously.) From the birth of the sun and moon to the berserkers of Valhalla to the eventual destruction and reformation of the nine worlds, the Norse Tradition tells of captivating gods and goddesses, of heroes and unmitigated disasters.

The pantheon of the Norse is large, like that of the Greeks, Romans and Egyptians. While some principal players such as Odin, Thor and Loki are well-fixed in the popular mindset, many others exist which are just as compelling. The Tradition of the Norse is filled with stories of valor and treachery, love and hatred, Valhalla and Hel. So, from the creation of the cosmos, according to the Norse, all the way through Ragnarök and beyond, I invite you to share this fascinating journey with me into one of the most iconic cultures the world has ever known.

Thanks again, I hope you enjoy it!

Martin R. Phillips

CHAPTER 1

Creation of the Cosmos, the World, and the Gods

It is first necessary to point out that, unlike most creation myths, in the Norse Religion—simply referred to by its adherents of old as "the tradition"—the creation of the cosmos and the destruction thereof was not a one-time deal. After Ragnarök, that is, the apocalyptic war in which many of the gods would be killed, the world would begin anew. I mention this here, because there are certain aspects of Ragnarök which are good to know throughout the creation myth, as it's something that the deities, demigods, etc. were aware of from the beginning. Ragnarök itself will be discussed in more detail later.

According to the Norse Tradition, the primordial universe was called Ginnungagap, the void (trans. gaping void.) Here, neither darkness nor light nor sound nor silence existed. Ginnungagap was immeasurably vast, said to extend in all directions infinitely (although, tradition also says that it was large enough to encompass a billion universes, had they existed. Either way, it was big—really, really big.)

From this primeval state of ultimately vast nothingness came two realms: Niflheimr ("house of mists,") the realm of ice, located in the north, and Muspelheimr (alternatively, Muspell; "home of desolation") the realm of fire located in the south of Ginnungagap.

Muspelheimr was a realm of eternally erupting volcanoes, thick, black smoke and flame. Winds blew smoke and volcanic exhaust throughout this realm. Muspelheimr was inhabited by the jötunn[1], Surtr, a fire-demon who wielded a sword of unmeasurable power in preparation for Ragnarök—more on him later.

Niflheimr was the land of ice and freezing rain. Just as vast and extreme a realm as Muspelheimr, Niflheimr was also home to unyielding winds, which blew frozen precipitation throughout its area. Niflheimr was also home to Hvergelmir, the primordial river (trans. bubbling/boiling spring,) and Élivágar, the primordial spring (trans. waves of ice.) From these sources, all of the waters in existence would come.

---

[1] *Plural: Jötnar. Translation/Definition: Devourer. Jötunn is often anglicized into "giant." Although the latter attribution is accurate to a point, it does tend to leave out the spirit of the Jötnar as "devourers of worlds," and so will be used sparingly within this text.*

Although the realms of Niflheimr and Muspelheimr were, initially, separate, over time, they both spread. It is where these forces of fire and ice would meet that is of primary concern to the tale.

Once the frigid materials of Niflheimr came into contact with the molten substances of Muspelheimr, a violent reaction occurred. The waters were thrown into the air, only to fall and mix with the incredibly hot elements below. From this process, the first of the jötnar was created. The jötunn was named Ymir (also referred to as Aurgelmir.)

The mixing of the fire and lava of Muspelheimr would continue to mix with the ice and water of Niflheimr, slowly melting that which was frozen and solidifying that which was molten.

Unlike most creation myths, Ymir, the first lifeform (other than Surtr, who seemed to spring out of the fires of Muspelheimr instantaneously,) laid without life for millennia. During this time, the composition of Ymir's body continued to form and mix together.

As Ymir's composition became more stable, he began to perspire. This perspiration formed the first of his children: a male and a female. After his feet mated with each other (now there's a mental picture,) another offspring was produced: a male, six-headed jötunn. These jötnar would become the progenitors of the gods.

Now, at the same time that Ymir was forming, and the ice and snow of Niflheimr melted from the heat of the lava and fire of Muspelheimr, another being came into existence: Auðumbla, a cow. Auðumbla, who received her nourishment through salt contained within the ice, would be the source of food for Ymir who suckled from the cow's teats.

As Auðumbla continued licking her way through the frozen-but-melting expanse, she began to lick the stones beneath the ice into the shape of a man; the first of the Aesir (also, Æsir) Gods: Buri. (Alternatively, some versions have her simply uncovering the already-formed god.)

From these beginnings, the ingredients and chief movers that would go on to create the gods, the worlds (all nine of them; more on that later) and all living things, were all present.

Now for a little genealogy (I'll try to keep it brief): Buri produced a son named Bor. Bolthorn, a jötunn, produced a daughter named Bestla. Bor and Bestla would marry and give birth to the Aesir gods Odin (aka Wodan, Woden, or Wotan,) Vili and Ve (or Vé.)

Theories diverge on what led to the confrontation which led to the death of Ymir at the hands of Odin and his siblings (some say that it was a matter of usurpation, others, a noise complaint levied against the jötunn that got a little out of hand,) however, the result is the same. The blood of the slain jötunn was so vast that it would end up drowning all but one frost ogre (a type of jötunn.) The surviving frost ogre, Bergelmir, survived by climbing into a boat called a lur (alternately, by swimming through the blood, towing his wife behind by the latter's hair.)

After killing Ymir, the three used different parts of the jötunn's body to create existence as the Norse saw it: The blood of Ymir was used to create the oceans, his flesh became the soil and primary substance of the earth, stones were fashioned from his teeth, trees from his hair, mountains from his bones, the sky from his skull and the clouds from his brains.

The sky was held aloft by four dwarves[2] named Nordri, Sudri, Austri, and Vestri[3]. Embers from Muspelheimr continued to float through the air, and so the three gods collected these and placed them in the skies to light the world.

The first humans were fashioned by Odin, Vili and Ve out of driftwood. The three gods bestowed upon humans gifts: Odin breathed life into them, Vili gave

---

[2] *The dwarves began life as maggots which grew within the slain body of Ymir. With the gift of knowledge and understanding by the gods to the dwarves, they would become the master smiths and hearty creatures which are often referenced in popular culture.*

[3] *If those names sound strangely familiar, but you're having a little trouble figuring out why, here's your answer: Nordri = North, Sudri = South, Austri = East and Vestri = West.*

them knowledge and Ve gave them their physical appearance and their senses. These humans were named Askr (or Ask) and Embla.

The world of mankind, created of the slain jötunn's body, was called Midgardr (or Midgard.) This land, though surrounded by the realm of giants (the Jötnar,) was protected by the three Aesirs by fashioning a fence from the jötunn's eyelashes.

Midgard was located between the primeval realms of Niflheimr and Muspelheimr. The other eight worlds were generally invisible to the inhabitants of Midgard, although there were times where other worlds could be perceived. One example of this is the connection between Midgard and Ásgardr (or Asgard,) the world of the gods, by a "rainbow bridge" called Bifrost.

So, we now have the world of the humans. As the other eight will be discussed to varying degrees later in the book, I'll forego a close inspection of each here. However, it is helpful to know what each of these worlds were and which beings would call them home. They are as follows:

Midgard was the world of humans.
Ásgardr was the world of the Aesir gods.
Vanaheimr was the world of the Vanir gods.
Jötunheimr was the world of the Jötnar.

Álfheimr[4] was the world of the elves.

Hel was the world of the dead or Náir[5].

Svartálfar was the world of the Dvergar or dwarves.

Niflheimr was the world of ice.

Muspelheimr was the world of fire and lava, home to Surtr.

Now, the stage is set. In the next chapter, we'll take a look at the major gods of Norse Tradition, and some of the important myths surrounding them.

---

[4] *Also called Ljosalfheimr, meaning "home of the light elves."*

[5] *Specifically, the evil, dishonored or unfit dead, as Valhalla—located within the realm of Asgard—was home to the honored dead. Think of Hel as we would think of hell; after all, it's the linguistic origin of the word.*

CHAPTER 2

The Aesir-Vanir War and the Mead of Poetry

The Aesir-Vanir War

Although the Norse Tradition was home to a large and rather diverse group of gods and other beings, two groups of gods, the Aesir and the Vanir, through their battle and subsequent armistice would change the landscape of the pantheon.

It all starts with a woman named Gullveig. Gullveig was a völva[6] and a practitioner of seidr (also called seid or seiðr,) a type of sorcery which was primarily in practice before the Christianization of modern-day Scandinavia. Seidr, while having many facets (most infamously a type of sex-magic,) was largely concerned with the divination and subsequent alteration of destiny.

The story begins with Gullveig making her way from place to place, world to world, plying her trade for the benefit (and gold) of various groups and individ-

---

[6] This is usually translated as "carrier of a wand" or similar.

uals. When she[7] reached Asgard, home of the Aesirs, she was an instant hit with the gods.

What happened next is fairly consistent throughout different sources, but the reasoning behind it is unclear; although there are a few theories.

In one version of the tale, the Aesirian gods, Odin in particular, are angered by the seeress's admonitions regarding the power structure chosen by the Aesirs. Gullveig, being favored by the Vanirs, was to the Aesirs, a representative of those gods.

In a similar version, the main cause of conflict was that the Aesirs had become (or had simply always been) the sole recipients of the tributes paid the gods by mankind, and it was the advice of the seeress that they, the Aesirs, either pay tribute to the Vanirs, or allow a portion of the tribute to go to the same.

In yet another version, the seeress is actually the goddess Freya, who, being a practitioner and goddess of seidr, herself, had so impressed the court of the Aesirs that the latter found themselves disgusted with their own greed and willingness to subvert their laws and loyalties. They blamed the seeress for their own lust for the power which they desired for its potential to empower them. While this particular version may

---

7 Commonly, she used the name "Gullveig Heidr," which roughly translates to "gleaming one" or "bright one."

explain the connection between the Vanirs and the seeress, it's not consistent with the Eddas.

Whatever the reason was, Odin shot his spear forth, striking, but not killing or inflicting permanent injury upon the woman. In their fury, the Aesirian gods stabbed the woman with their spears and burnt her alive not once, not twice, but three times. Each time, Gullveig would resurrect from the ashes. This did not make the Aesirians happy.

When they couldn't kill the seeress, tensions began to build between the two groups of gods. At first, the Vanirs and the Aesirs tried to work out a diplomatic solution, but this ended in an impasse. The war itself isn't explained in much detail, although, commonly, it's stated that neither group could win definitive victory against the other. While the Aesirs fought by more conventional means, the Vanirs used sorcery and subterfuge as their method of attack.

It finally became apparent that neither group was likely to ever triumph over the other. So, they came together to forge a truce. It is with the truce and that which followed it that the Eddas were concerned.

The Prose Edda explains that, as a traditional show of unity and peace between the Aesirs and Vanirs, the two groups met and took turns spitting into a cauldron or vat. One of the things about the substances (even something as seemingly insignificant as saliva) of gods is that they're never mundane.

Rather than simply dumping out the vat and possibly offending one another, they decided to put the swishing fluid to good use. Therefore, from their intermingling saliva, they created a man named Kvasir.

Kvasir and the Mead of Poetry

Now, being created from god-spit may not sound like the most promising of beginnings, but Kvasir was considered as quite possibly the wisest being (certainly the wisest human) in creation. It was written that there was no question for which he couldn't provide an insightful, practical answer.

The Aesirs and Vanirs had learned their lesson about trying to take from or overthrow one another, and so Kvasir was allowed to roam freely. He travelled throughout Midgard, spreading knowledge and wisdom to all that he met.

One day, he came across two dwarves: Fjalar and Galar. These dwarves were, unbeknownst to the Kvasir, quite the murderous, anti-intellectual beings. They quickly killed Kvasir and collected his blood. As he was so endowed with wisdom, this virtue remained within his vital fluid. The two boiled it in the magic cauldron Odhrorir, and mixed it with honey (alternately, they enlist the giant Suttungr to add the nectar to the blood.) When approached about the fate of Kvasir, the dwarves said that he had choked (or suffocated) on his own intelligence. For two beings that harbored such distaste for intelligence and knowledge, the reply was really quite clever.

The mixture of blood and honey became "The Mead of Poetry." Any who would drink of the fluid would gain the knowledge and understanding to become a poet or a scholar. This was safe enough in the hands of the dwarves, as, due to their anti-intellectualism, they didn't have the desire to partake of it. However, it would be their lust for killing that would take the Mead of Poetry from their hands.

When the two decided that killing the wisest man hadn't properly slaked their bloodlust, they went before the giant Gilling and offered to take him for a ride on their boat. (It must have been a rather large vessel.) Once at sea, the murderous pair capsized the boat and watched as Gilling drowned in the depths of the ocean.

As an act of anything but contrition, the two returned to the home of Gilling and informed his wife of her husband's death. While Fjalar offered to take Gilling's wife to visit the spot of her husband's death (no doubt to dump her in the same spot,) Galar was growing weary of the wife's sobbing. The second voyage was scrapped and the dwarves simply dispatched Gilling's wife as she passed through the doorway of her home by dropping a millstone on her head.

The two psychotic dwarves rejoiced, but their mirth would be short-lived. For when Suttungr (a son of the murdered couple. Although not necessarily relevant to the rest of the story, he was rather drunk at the time. Alcohol and the ensuing drunkenness thereof was a fairly common occurrence in the stories of Norse Mythology) found out, he tracked the pair down and snatched them. He took them to a reef at low tide, with the full intention of letting the two drown in the very waters in which his father had.

The two dwarves, seeing Hel in their immediate future, quickly offered the jötunn the Mead of Poetry in exchange for their lives. Suttungr took the mead back to his home, the mountain Hnitbjörg, and placed it under the watchful eye of his daughter, Gunnlöd.

<u>Odin</u>

While there will be a great deal more about Odin throughout this book, as he was the chief deity of the Aesirs, he does play yet another role in the story of the Mead of Poetry.

Odin, along with being the chief deity of the Aesirs, was also a god of knowledge, royalty, berserker fury, battle, death, the arts (specifically language: the runic alphabet and poetry,) healing and sorcery—although other attributions do exist, varying a bit from source to source. His wife was the goddess Frigg, with whom he bore Baldur (also Balder, Baldr,) Hod and Hermud; with Jord: Thor; with Rind: Váli (alternately, Valie); with the jötunn, Grid: Vidar (who would slay Fenrir the wolf, more on that later.) Odin had an eight-legged horse, Sleipnir, which was the fastest creature extant, and was capable of travelling between the nine worlds with ease.

Now, Odin was tireless when it came to the search for further knowledge and wisdom. When he became aware of the Mead of Poetry and its location within Hnitbjörg, he set out to claim it for his own. In order to do this, he employed quite the clever (if rather brutal) deception.

He began by traveling to the home of Baugi, the younger brother of Suttungr, disguised as a common farmer. Upon his arrival, he found nine farmhands tending to the fields. The god offered to sharpen the farmhands' scythes for them, and the workers agreed.

Being the chief deity of, well, pretty much everything, he was able to sharpen the farmers' scythes with such deft effectiveness that the men implored him to sell them the whetstone he had used. Odin agreed, but rather than simple trade or barter, the god tossed the whetstone into the air and, before it fell to the ground, the workers killed one another with the very scythes the deity had just sharpened.

Upon making his way to the house of Baugi, he was offered shelter for the night. While there, the jötunn shared his frustration at the mutual killing of his workers. Odin, not quite magnanimously, offered to work the fields in the farmhands' stead... for a price. The price was a sip of the mead which Baugi's brother had come to possess. The jötunn hesitantly agreed, and Odin—by this point, calling himself Bölverkr so as to not expose his true identity—set to work.

Odin worked through the summer and the fall. When winter finally came, Odin asked about his payment. He and Baugi went to Hnitbjörg to convince Suttungr to allow the gracious farmhand to wet his lips with the Mead of Poetry.

Baugi should have checked with his brother before offering some of the mead as payment, though, as Suttungr refused. Odin, being quite the persuasive type, convinced Baugi to help him reach the mead through other means, namely, by boring through the mountain and into the dwelling of Gunnlöd, the guardian of the mead.

Odin gave the jötunn a drill with which to bore through the mountain. Baugi initially tried to deceive him by only drilling partway through, but Odin discovered the ruse by blowing into the hole, causing the dust and debris to come out the top of the hole. Once the god had convinced the jötunn to fulfill his end of the bargain, he repeated his test, this time, satisfied that Baugi had, indeed followed through.

Odin changed his form into that of a snake and slithered his way through the hole. Although Baugi promptly tried to stab him with the auger, the Aesir made it through unscathed.

Once inside, Odin morphed into the figure of a young, attractive man and set to work making an arrangement with Gunnlöd. The arrangement was that if she would give him three sips of the mead, Odin would share Gunnlöd's bed for three consecutive nights. Being that Odin had turned himself into quite the handsome rogue, Gunnlöd agreed.

After three nights with Gunnlöd, Odin persisted regarding the mead. Gunnlöd took him to the chamber where the mead was stored. The draught was contained within three vessels. Odin took a drink from each, but rather than a sip, he consumed the entirety of the Mead of Poetry.

Not being one to stick around and gloat, Odin transformed himself into an eagle and flew off in the direction of Asgard. Suttungr quickly came to discover what had happened and gave chase, turning himself into an eagle. Odin would prove too fast for him, though. As the god approached Asgard, the other Aesirs saw the chase and set vats of their own along the border of the realm.

Odin quickly regurgitated the mead into the vessels, but the closing proximity of the giant forced the god to be a bit hasty. A few drops of the Mead of Poetry fell from his mouth (or, in this case, beak,) and landed in Midgard, the realm of humanity.

Suttungr retreated, as he was outnumbered. The drops which fell to Midgard were available for the consumption of any, but lacked sufficient quantity to do its full work. It's from these drops, the Norse believed, that those mediocre in poetry and/or scholarship gained their lackluster "inspiration." The rest of the Mead of Poetry, however, was doled out by Odin himself, empowering his fellow gods along with his favored poets and scholars to untold heights of genius.

Thus, what started as the first war in Norse Tradition eventually gave rise to new apexes of poetic and scholarly work. I can't help but wonder if Odin gave some of this draught to the authors of the Eddas.

CHAPTER 3

Freyja, Loki and Thor, Myths and Legends

The pantheon of Norse Mythology (Tradition) is vast, filled with gods and demigods of varying powers and temperaments. After the Vanir-Aesir War, the two camps came together and, for the most part, worked famously with one another. That said, there is plenty to learn about the deities, and thus, the Norse conception of life, the world and the cosmos.

As some of the more poignant stories regarding the individual gods are of their interactions with one another, in this chapter, it serves well to not only include stories of the individual deities, but to introduce and include other gods pertinent to their stories.

Freyja, Loki and Thor:

Freyja and the Disappearance of Óðr

Freyja (alternately, Freya,) was a Vanir, a daughter of Njord and his wife Nerthus (who was also Njord's sister.) Freya was the twin sister to Freyr. Freya was a goddess of many things, including beauty, fertility, sexuality, luxury, death and war. She was also a goddess of seidr. Her consort was Óðr (possibly an early form of the name Odin.) Her day is Fredag (Friday.)

Before her husband, Óðr left (more on that in a moment,) the two had two daughters named Hnoss and Gersemi[8]. Now, Óðr, whose name commonly translates into "the wanderer," or "the frenzied one," although many other attributions of the name do exist. Not much is generally known of Óðr himself, apart from his connection with Freyja.

One day, Óðr simply vanished. While it's unknown exactly where he went or what happened to him after he left[9], Óðr's departure had a rather profound effect on Freyja. She tried to find or follow him, weeping, along her way.

---

[8] Both names meaning "jewel" or "gem."

[9] It is, however, theorized that Óðr simply traveled from land to land, though always out of the reach of his wife.

Freyja was the most desired of the goddesses with gods, Jötnar and men. Her propensity toward lust once got her into quite the row with Loki.

Loki and the Art of Not Keeping One's Mouth Shut

Loki was the son of Fárbauti and Laufey, and brother to Helblindi and Býleistr. Some testimonies refer to him as a god, others as a jötunn[10], while others claim him as being both. He was a mischievous being, and was just as likely to hinder the gods as to help them.[11]

Now, Loki was kind of a jerk. At one gathering, thrown by the god Ægir, Loki became furious at the servants of Ægir, named Fimafeng and Eldir, for being so kind and accommodating toward the other gods, who he saw as being corrupt and unworthy of praise[12]. To make his point, Loki killed Fimafeng.

Regardless the reason for Loki's jealousy, the gods didn't stand for this act and chased him from the hall.

---

[10] Likely due to his sexual relationship with the jötunn Angrboða; the union of which produced Jörmungandr, the World Serpent (see chapter five,) the wolf Fenrir and the goddess Hel.

[11] One of the central myths of Loki is his involvement in the death of Baldur; this will be discussed in the following chapter.

[12] Or, in some versions, that Loki was infuriated by the kindness of the gods toward these servants, who he, again, saw as being unworthy of the praise.

He retreated into the woods for a time and the gods went back to their mead.

Upon his return, Loki accosted the remaining servant, Eldir. Although he left Eldir alive, the gods weren't about to allow Loki to return into the hall. In response to this, Loki invoked the oath sworn by Odin that the two would drink with one another, and Odin allowed the trickster god back to the table.

While a god with a little more humility, or at least a little more tact, may not have tried to push his luck, Loki began insulting the gods. He claimed that the gods were weak and sexually promiscuous. Freyja, being particularly offended by this, challenges Loki, saying that the latter was mad to be so vitriolic in the presence of the goddess Frigg, as Frigg knew the future and fate of all.

Loki snapped back, accusing Freyja of having lain with every god and elf in the hall[13]. The row goes on for quite some time.

Another myth involves Freyja, Loki and (let's be honest, you've been waiting for him to make an appearance,) Thor (Þórr in the original Norse.) First though, it bears telling how Thor's hammer came into existence.

---

[13] This may or may not have been an accurate accusation, given Freyja's love of, well, love.

Loki and the Creation of Thor's Hammer

Thor's iconic hammer, Mjölnir, was forged by the dwarves Brokkr and Sindri, as part of a bet with Loki. In this bet, Loki literally bet his head that the two dwarves couldn't make anything more stunning or functional than the Sons of Ivaldi—famous for such things as Odin's spear or lance, Gungir. The two were sucked into the challenge and set about constructing a hammer.

Sindri worked the forge and Brokkr, the bellows. Sindri instructed Brokkr that, under no circumstances was the latter to stop working the bellows until he (Sindri) had finished his part of the work and removed it from the forge.

Now, as already stated, Loki was kind of a jerk. During the first portion of the work, Sindri placed pig leather into the forge. As Sindri worked, Brokkr manned the bellows. All was fine until Loki turned himself into a biting fly in an attempt to get the dwarf to pause just long enough to ruin the material. Loki, as a fly, bit Brokkr hard on the hand, but the dwarf persisted in his duties.

Sindri finished his first item: A boar, Gullinbursti, which the dwarves would offer to the god Freyr. Gullinbursti was capable of running through water and air with more swiftness than any steed may, and the boar's bristles and mane were of such shimmering gold that darkness would retreat in its presence.

Next, Sindri placed gold into the forge and, again, set to work. Loki, undaunted by his previous failure to flummox Brokkr, returned again, this time biting the dwarf hard on the neck. As before, though, the dwarf didn't flinch.

When Sindri had finished, he removed the finished product from the forge: The magical ring, Draupnir, which, every ninth night, would produce eight more rings, identical in size, shape and quality. This ring, the dwarves gave to Odin.

Finally, Sindri set to work on the final artifact by placing iron into the forge. Loki again landed on Brokkr, this time biting him deeply on the eyelid. While the dwarf could withstand the pain, he stopped working the bellows for the briefest of moments as he wiped the blood from his eye.

When Sindri had finished with the third and final item, the hammer Mjölnir, the handle was shorter than intended, due to Brokkr's failure to keep the bellows going continuously. This is why Thor's hammer, despite its depictions in modern-day media, could only be wielded with one hand.

Although Loki had succeeded in getting Brokkr to stop working the forge, if only for an instant, it was clear that the dwarves had won the bet. Loki, never one to lose graciously, protested by saying that, though the two had a right to his head, in order to take it, they would have to separate it from his neck. As cutting or otherwise damaging his neck wasn't part of the bargain, Loki convinced the dwarves to leave Loki's head where it was.

That's not to say that the dwarves were happy about it. Though they were unable to take Loki's head, Brokkr—undoubtedly with some satisfaction—sewed Loki's mouth shut with wire as a lesson in not making bets that can't be paid.

The Theft of Thor's Hammer

Thor was the god of thunder, lightning and storms in general. Other attributions include him as the god of strength, the defender of humanity, healing and oak trees among others. He was the son of Odin and Jord (or Jörð; Earth.) His day is Thor's Day, or, more modernly, Thursday. He was a redhead who, despite the fact he was rather slow-witted, was fierce in battle.

After receiving his hammer from the dwarves, Thor awoke one morning to find that the weapon had gone missing. As stated before, Loki was kind of a jerk and Thor knew this. He assumed that the hammer was taken by Loki and went before the miscreant god, demanding that Mjölnir be returned.

Loki, however, persisted that he had nothing to do with the theft; although, he told Thor, he had a pretty good idea who did the deed. In order to for Loki to reach the culprit, Thor implored Freyja, asking her to let Loki borrow her cloak, made of the feathers of falcons, so that he may regain his hammer. Freyja assented, and Loki, lifted by the cloak (specifically, its ability to grant its wearer the power of flight,) travelled to Jötunheimr.

Once he'd arrived, he came across the jötunn, Thrymr (Þrymr in the original Norse.) Thrymr quickly admitted to having taken the hammer and hiding it some-where below the earth, at or around a depth of eight miles. He was so fast to make his confession because he wanted something in return: He wanted the most beautiful of the goddesses as his wife. In other words, he wanted Freyja in exchange for Thor's hammer.

Earlier in this chapter, we learned how Freyja was the most desired of the goddesses, and was known for "spreading the love," but she was far from being without standards. When Loki returned to Thor with the jötunn's demand, and Thor, subsequently, went before Freyja to beg her to go through with the jö-tunn's demands, she snorted, flatly refusing to marry the jötunn.

With Freyja unwilling to become the concubine of the treacherous giant, the gods came together to figure out how to get the hammer back as, without it, the Jötnar were likely to use it to attack (and likely lay waste) to Asgard. Heimdall, a god with nine mothers (let that sink in for a minute,) finally suggested a bold plan: For Thor to dress as Freyja and go before the jötunn himself in order to retrieve his hammer.

Thor, reluctantly, agreed and was thus dressed in the garments of Freyja, right down to her necklace and keys. Loki, never wanting to miss out on much, de-cided to ride with Thor, posing as a bridesmaid. Thrymr saw the disguised gods approaching and became overwhelmed with excitement, having his servants quickly get to work preparing for the wedding.

Once at the wedding reception, Thor didn't hold his cover very well, as he devoured eight salmon, an ox (the whole ox) and enough mead to drop a detachment of Vikings. Thrymr, though rather impressed, began to grow a little suspicious. Loki explained that Freyja had been so enamored with the idea of wedding Thrymr that, in preparation for the wedding, she had fasted for eight days[14].

Thrymr finally got tired of waiting to plant a kiss on his new "bride." When he lifted the veil, the jig would have been up if it weren't for Loki's penchant for trickery. He explained "the bride's" fiery eyes by saying that she hadn't slept in eight days, also in preparation for the wedding.

Things came to a head, though, when Thrymr sets Mjölnir in Thor's lap as per his agreement with Loki. With his hammer now in hand, Thor tore his disguise asunder and slaughtered not only Thrymr, but the other jötnar who had attended the wedding.

---

[14] See Little Red Riding Hood.

CHAPTER 4

Central Myths, Legends and Stories

With so many gods and even more legends, Norse Tradition is a treasure-trove of interesting tales regarding the gods and the worlds. One of the most interesting tales is that of Odin and Mimir, and that's where this chapter begins.

Odin and Mimir

Mimir ("the wise one,") was unparalleled in his wisdom and advice, save, possibly for Kvasir. Mimir had a spring or a well, called Mimisbrunnr, which contained the waters of wisdom.

As we've seen, Odin was always on the lookout for a way to increase his knowledge and perspicacity, and so, when Mimir asked him to leave one of his eyes as payment for partaking of the waters, Odin did so, gladly.

The following are three tales of Odin and his quest for, and attainment of, wisdom.

How Mimir Lost His Head

The association of Odin and Mimir would not end there, though. After the Aesir-Vanir War, the two camps sent members of their ranks as hostages to the other in the Norse tradition. The Aesirs sent to the Vanir were Hoenir and Mimir[15][16].

---

[15] The Vanir sent Freyja, her brother Freyr and their father Njord to the Aesirs. This is how the Vanir Freyja became a member of the Aesir camp.

[16] In another version of this tale, Mimir was simply killed in the battle between the Aesirs and Vanirs. What happened after his beheading, however, generally remains consistent.

While in Vanaheim, home of the Vanirs, Hoenir quickly became regarded as a source of indomitable wisdom, or at least, that's what they thought. Hoenir was simply regurgitating the words of Mimir, but the ruse continued.

Now, while Mimir held wisdom beyond the ages, Hoenir was much less schooled. While Mimir was with Hoenir, the latter appeared to be a sage, but once Mimir had left Hoenir's side things unraveled rather quickly.

After Hoenir copped out of answering difficult questions one too many times, simply repeating, "Let others decide," the Vanir cut Mimir's head off, claiming that they'd been swindled and that the exchange of hostages hadn't been fair. To show their disapproval further, they sent Mimir's head back to the Aesirs.

Upon finding this, Odin was distraught. Mimir had been a friend and a trusted advisor to him, and so he preserved the head. Despite being decapitated, Mimir continued to offer Odin advice as a literal talking head.

Odin and the Runes

The Runic language of the Norse is fascinating. Runes were not simple pictorial or literary depictions of letters or words, but were intrinsically principles of power.

Odin was drawn to discovering these runes, but the process by which he would have to go to uncover them is right up there in self-mutilation for the sake of knowledge (if not simply humiliation with a nice payoff at the end) with the act of plucking out his own eye.

Odin, in furthering his quest for wisdom, travelled to the Well of Urd, the home of runic knowledge. The runes wouldn't just show themselves to anyone—not even a god like Odin—whoever sought them had to prove themselves worthy of their power.

In order to show his worth and his tenacity, Odin hung himself from the world tree, Yggdrasil, stabbing himself in the side with his own lance. He would remain there for nine days, turning away any offers of aid from the other gods. During this time, Odin came close to death, but managed to live long enough for the runes to reveal themselves to him; his sacrifice had been accepted.

Once in possession of the knowledge of the runes, Odin freed himself from Yggdrasil and carried his knowledge back to the gods and, subsequently, mankind.

The Battle of Wits: A Final Tale of Odin's Wisdom

While this portion of Norse lore happened after the death of Baldur (discussed later in the chapter,) it bears stating here.

Odin once set out to prove his sapience, by challenging a powerful seeress, named Vathruthnir. In order to protect his true identity, Odin donned disguise. The two would engage one another in a battle of wits[17]. As the exchange holds useful information about the Norse beliefs, a portion of this back-and-forth will be included, however briefly, here.

The seeress began the questioning, by asking Odin the names of the horses that drew the day and the night, respectively through the sky. Odin answered that the horses were Hrimfaxi, the drawer of the night; while Skinfaxi pulled the day.

Odin then asked Vathruthnir about the origins of the sun and the moon. To this, the seeress correctly responded that they were the children of the jötunn, Mundilfäri. The daughter, Sól, pulled the sun while Máni, Mundilfäri's son, drove the moon.

The two went back and forth for quite some time, each proving worthy in their knowledge of the worlds and its inhabitants.

---

[17] In some tellings, the loser of the bout would be killed.

It wasn't until Gagnráðr asked the seeress what Odin said to his son Baldur before setting him adrift in the Norse funerary tradition   that his cover was blown.

Vathruthnir concluded that the only one who would know the answer to that would be Odin, but conceded that the latter had proven his superior wisdom.

The Tale of Sigurd and the Dragon

Not all important tales in mythology relate to Odin or, indeed, the gods themselves directly. The tale of Sigurd is one such myth, which is of particular relevance to the Norse Tradition.

Sigurd was the son of Sigmund and Hiordis. He was born after his father's death at the hands of a disguised Odin who, having already killed Sigmund, shattered the fallen hero's sword to pieces. Hiordis would go on to bear her late husband's son, giving him the pieces of the sword his father had once carried.

Sigurd, often held to be a distant descendant of Odin, would be raised—partially by his mother and her new husband, the king Alf, but largely by Regin, who became his foster-father. It was Regin who would re-forge the sword of Sigurd's fallen father, Sigmund.

Regin had a bit of a complicated history, as he had once been denied his share of gold at the killing of the dwarf, Ótr (also Otr, Ottar, Otter,) his brother. One day, while Otr was swimming in a pool at the base of a waterfall with the dwarf Andvari. In order to do this without her being any the wiser, Otr would don the form of, you guessed it, an otter.

One day, Otr was swimming in the pool when Loki (you just know something bad is about to happen) spotted the creature and, not knowing that the otter was actually Otr in disguise, slayed him. Loki went to show his prize to the king of the dwarves, Hreidmar. Unbeknownst to Loki, Hreidmar was the father of Otr, Regin and Fafnir (more on him in a minute.) The two brothers detained Loki, demanding recompense for their slain brother.

Loki, never one to pay his debts honestly, captured Andvari, the dwarf, and demanded her gold. This she gave, but among the bullion was a ring[18] that would bring dire misfortune to any who wore it. Loki brought the treasure to the bereaved brothers and stuffed Otr's body with it before covering the same with the rest of the gold. He left the ring atop the pile. Shortly thereafter, though, Fafnir killed his father and cut his brother out of his share of the gold.

Back to Sigurd: Regin approached Sigurd one day, telling him that he needed to choose a horse for himself. Sigurd set out to do this and, fortuitously, came across Odin on his way, the latter, in disguise. Odin divined the young man's purpose and told him that the best way to choose his horse would be to chase a band of horses into a river, selecting only the one that swam successfully to the other side as his own. Sigurd did this, and this is how he ended up with his

---

[18] See The Ring of the Nibelungen by Wagner.

horse: A direct descendant of Odin's own steed, Sleipnir.

After Sigurd had his steed, Regin approached him again, telling Sigurd about how his brother, Fafnir, had stolen the gold, literally from his dead brother Otr's body. He also informed him that, due to the ring's cursed power, Fafnir had become a dragon, and that the best way to slay him would be to dig a hole, climb into and cover it to lie in wait for Fafnir to come near. Sigurd listened to this advice, and was also counseled by Odin, again disguised, to dig a trench in addition to the hole in order to capture the slain dragon's blood.

Regin went about forging Sigurd a sword, but when the latter went to test the blade by striking the anvil with it, the weapon splintered in his hand. Regin forged another, but this one also cracked. As they say, though, the third time's the charm. Sigurd brought the fragments of his father's sword to Regin, who re-forged it into a working blade, called Gram (alternately, Gramr.) When Sigurd went to test this blade, not the sword, but the anvil split with the blow. He was now ready to do battle.

Sigurd went to the dwelling of Fafnir and made the necessary preparations. Once lying in wait, Sigurd heard the mighty beast approaching and, at just the right moment, he leapt forth, killing Fafnir.

The blood drained into the trenches and Sigurd bathed in it. This gave him the ability to understand the language of the birds[19], which proceeded to warn him that his mentor, Regin, had also been corrupted by the ring and was plotting Sigurd's demise.

When Sigurd returned, gold in tow, he didn't hesitate in killing Regin. While this wouldn't be the end of the ring, it brought the chapter of Regin and Fafnir to a close.

---

[19] Alternately, he consumed Fafnir's heart at this point, which gave him this power.

CHAPTER 5

Central Myths and Legends: Ragnarök

Ragnarök

Though it was debatable whether to include Ragnarök in this chapter, or to place it in Morality, Life &
Death and the Practical Enactment of the Mythos in
Norse Life[20], it is far too crucial to the Norse Tradition
to hold back further.

Ragnarök is, in Norse Tradition, a cataclysmic event
on the level that would have a devastating effect on
all of the nine worlds. Like many mythologies, Ragnarök is prophesied from the beginning. In fact, the
gods—even, perhaps especially, Surtr who was sharp-
ening his doom blade before other gods even came
into being—are, in one way or another, constantly
preparing for this final battle.

As it is prophesized in the Eddas, the pantheon of
Norse gods, jötnar, elves, Valkyries and others even
knew which way the battle would go, who would die

---

[20] Chapter Six

and at whose hands. The main indication that Ragnarök would be imminent was that there would be three winters in a row without summer dividing them. Despite all of this, the beings refused to sit back and let prophecy run its course.

Key Players in Ragnarök: Jörmungandr

Jörmungandr (also Jǫrmungandr or Jormungand) was a giant, four-legged serpent that surrounded the world of Midgard. Often referred to as the Midgard Serpent or the World Serpent, Jörmungandr would play a vital role in the events of Ragnarök.

Jörmungandr was one of the children of Loki by the jötunn Angrboda[21], and was of such massive size that it encircled the world of Midgardr entirely. A sea-serpent, Jörmungandr was so large, in fact, that its mouth closed over its own tail. It was said that when Jörmungandr opened its mouth, so would begin Ragnarök.

Jörmungandr was the arch rival of Thor, who, in an attempt to kill the serpent, lowered a fishing line, hooking Jörmungandr. Thor attempted to raise the creature from its depths, but when the jötunn, Hymir, saw the scene, he severed the line in fear that Thor was unwittingly about to call forth Ragnarök.

This wouldn't be the final conflict between the two, though. During Ragnarök, Jörmungandr would open its mouth, poisoning the sky. During the heat of the battle, Thor would slay the mighty serpent, only to

---

[21] The other two being Hel and Fenrir.

fall dead after taking nine steps, having been poisoned by Jörmungandr.

Key Players in Ragnarök: Fenrir, the Wolf

Fenrir was a great wolf, son of Loki and the jötunn Angrboda. Now, the events of Ragnarok had been foretold, and so the gods were well aware that, unless they could prevent it, Fenrir would come to kill Odin during the final battle.

Although it was also told that Odin's death would be avenged, the gods set out to change the course of destiny. Sadly, this doesn't usually work, even in mythology.

What the gods did was to attempt to raise the wolf, themselves, hopefully persuading him to align himself with them at the coming of Ragnarök. This plan changed, though, when the gods witnessed the incredible rate of growth of the mighty creature. Their next gambit was to bind Fenrir, rendering him harmless to Odin and the other gods.

The gods, knowing that Fenrir wouldn't submit to this measure voluntarily, went to the wolf, telling him that they wanted to play a game—one which would test his strength. Fenrir agreed, and so allowed the gods to chain him up. He quickly burst through the bonds, proud of his might.

The gods tried again, this time, using a heavier chain, but again, Fenrir broke the bonds without much hassle.

It wasn't until the gods implored the dwarves to create the strongest chains ever created that they had a chance to incapacitate their future foe. The chain was very strong, but was also very light, even soft to the touch. Fenrir, sensing that something was off, said that he would only agree to be bound if one of the gods would place his or her hand in his mouth; thus, if the "game" was, indeed a trick, the gods would pay for their treachery.

As this surely meant that someone was going to lose a hand, the gods were hesitant. Tyr[22] (or Týr,) the god of glory, law and justice finally stepped forward, offering his own hand in exchange for the wolf's trust. Once bound, Fenrir struggled against the chains, but was unable to free himself. He bit the hand from Tyr's body, but he was already bound, unable to move or free himself.

The Death of Baldur, and the Coming of Ragnarök

Baldur was the son of Odin and his wife Frigg. A god of wholesomeness and light, Baldur was much beloved among the gods.

---

[22] Tyr's day is now commonly called Tuesday.

Little is known of Loki's motivation, although it is posited that he hated Baldur for his supposed invulnerability (which will be discussed presently,) but what is told in the Tradition is that Loki would have the beloved god killed.

It all started when Baldur had a prophetic dream about some great tragedy which was to befall him. Frightened for his son, Odin swiftly made his way to the land of the dead where dwelled a powerful, but deceased, jötunn seeress named Vafþrúðnir (or Vathruthnir/Vathrudnir.)

Upon Odin's arrival, he took on a disguise, calling himself Gagnráðr, and woke the seeress. Finding the seeress's dwelling festooned with decorations, Odin asked Vathruthnir for what purpose the feast was to be held. She immediately responded that Baldur would be arriving soon. This may not have been too shocking a statement, if it weren't for the fact that the hall was in the land of the dead. The seeress had just confirmed that Odin's son, Baldur, wasn't long for the world of the gods of Asgard. The seeress did tell Odin, though, that Baldur would be resurrected after Ragnarök.

Odin returned to Valhalla, his hall within Asgard (much more on that later,) with the news that Baldur was to be killed, Frigg travelled far and wide, making every living thing take an oath that they would not kill or harm Baldur... Everything, that is, except for mistletoe, which the goddess saw as being too in-nocuous a thing to take such an oath. I think we can see where this is going.

The gods rejoiced in Baldur's new imperviousness to harm. They even went so far as to entertain them-selves by hurling objects at the god, and watching them fall away, leaving Baldur completely unfazed.

Loki, upon seeing this, was overcome with a fit of jealousy. He disguised himself and went before Frigg, asking her if she had actually convinced every living thing to take the oath not to harm her son. Frigg proudly stated that she had, with the exception of mistletoe, as it was too small and pure to hurt any-one. That was the nail in Baldur's proverbial coffin.

Now armed with the information that mistletoe was the only substance which could possibly cause Baldur harm, Loki collected an amount of it and made a spear from it. He then returned to Asgard, spear in hand, and approached Hod, the blind brother of Bal-dur.

Although by accident on the part of Hod, the spear was thrust into Baldur's body, killing him. The gods were shocked. Odin and the jötunn conceived and bore Váli, who grew to full measure within a day of his birth. Once Váli was at full strength, he killed Hod.

Baldur was interned by being set upon a funeral pyre, borne upon a ship. The pyre was set aflame, but Baldur wouldn't be the only one upon it, as his wife, Nanna threw herself into the flames[23].

Loki's treachery wasn't over, though. Frigg sent Hermud to try and strike a bargain with Hel to release Baldur from the realm of the dead. Hel, who was joined at the time by a rather morose Baldur, said that if the dead god was so beloved, then every living thing would weep for him, and it was only on the fulfillment of this condition that Hel would agree to return Baldur to Asgard.

The message went out to every creature in all of the worlds, and all wept at the loss of Baldur. All, that is, but Loki, disguised as the jötunn, Thökk (Þökk in the Old Norse.) Having failed, by virtue of Loki's continued duplicity, Baldur was doomed to remain in Hel, with Hel, until after Ragnarök, when he would be resurrected to rule over all. With Baldur's death, and the gods' failure to retrieve him from Hel, the first step in the prophecy of Ragnarök had been fulfilled.

---

[23] Alternately, she died of grief and was then set upon the pyre with her husband.

The Binding of Loki, The Final Battle and the Next Beginning

Loki, having finally been discovered for his part in the scheme, fled Asgard. In order to evade his would-be captors, Loki went to the pool at the base of a waterfall and, having turned himself into a salmon, swam within the stream.

As he emerged in order to fashion a net—in order to capture food—by the light of a fire, Odin, though only one-eyed, spotted him in the distance. Loki divined that the Aesir gods were on his trail, and so he leapt back into the water as a salmon, having cast his net into the fire.

Upon finding the fire, and in it, the net, the gods fashioned their own net to catch Loki. He successfully evaded them, time and time again, but was finally caught by Thor as the former leapt from the water, trying to escape.

Now in the gods' hands, Loki was bound with the entrails of his son, Nari, who had been slain by his other son, Narfi[24] who had been transformed into a wolf. The entrails were turned to iron by the gods,

---

[24] In some tellings, Nari and Narfi are the same being, and the one who was transformed into the wolf was his son, Váli; not to be confused with Odin's son of the same name

but that wasn't enough punishment for the one who had slain Baldur and, quite literally, brought about the Norse apocalypse. Above his head was hung a venomous snake which dripped poison onto the bound god's face.

With Loki and Fenrir both bound, the gods enjoyed a moment of relief, but Ragnarök was already on its way.

Three roosters crowed[25]: One in the forest Gálgviðr, located in Jötunheim, one in Asgard and the last in Hel. Heimdall, keeper of the Gjallarhorn, an instrument whose sole purpose was to announce the onset of Ragnarök, raised the instrument and sounded the alarm. The world tree, Yggdrasil quaked, and Jörmungandr thrashed, his enormity causing enormous waves to rise and crash.

Surtr came from the south, wielding his sword, and the jötnar advanced on Asgard. The Valkyries—whose job it was to select the bravest of the fallen warriors of humanity, one half of which dwell in a state of constant battle in Valhalla, preparing for Ragnarök[26] — prepared for the onslaught of the jötnar. Meanwhile, the people of Midgard grew ever more destructive toward one another. Perhaps worst of all

---

[25] See the denial of Christ by Peter.

[26] The other half of the honored dead being led to Freyja. More on this in chapter six.

(with the exception of Surtr's presence,) Loki and Fenrir broke free of their bonds, the former leading the charge against the Aesirs aboard the ship of the dead. The sky went dark, as the stars disappeared, and Fenrir ran with his lower jaw dragging the ground, his upper jaw above the sky, consuming everything in his path, including the sun and the moon.

The battle was joined, and Odin was almost immediately consumed by Fenrir, as was Tyr. As foretold, Vidar avenged his father's death by taking the wolf by the jaws and hyper-extending to the point of breakage, finally stabbing the great wolf through the heart.

Freyr and Surtr joined battle with one another, with the bout ending in both of their deaths. Also, Loki met his end at the hands of Heimdall, but not before the former had inflicted a mortal wound upon the latter; thus, they too, killed each other.

Jörmungandr, having released his own tail, rose to Asgard, his mouth open as he unleashed his venom into the air. Thor would kill the serpent, but not before being poisoned himself. He, too, fell dead.

As most of the gods lay dead, the nine worlds sank once more into the water and the nothingness of Ginnungagap reigned once more. Unlike many end-of-times myths, though, the worlds would not be lost forever.

In time, all was recreated with Baldur in charge. All became green and full of life as before. Humanity, which had nearly been eliminated entirely, would be reborn with Lifthrasir and Lif, this time playing the role that Askr and Embla had once played after the first creation of the cosmos. The sun and moon, now the descendants of their predecessors returned to the sky, and all was made new once more.

CHAPTER 6

Morality, Life and Death

Morality to the Norse was, in many ways, akin to those of other polytheistic religions, specifically that of the Greeks and the Romans. Rather than the ascetic nature of the monotheistic religion(s), the gods of the Norse espoused things found in nature. They, like the people who revered them, were often flawed. They could be quick to anger, or to cheat or to deceive or kill. But even those more insidious gods, such as Loki, had their shining moments.

The Norse viewed everything in nature as being attributed to one god or another; or at least some other being or type of being, such as the dwarves or the elves, etc. When a storm rolled in, it was viewed as being Thor's hammer crashing down. Therefore, while the Norse strived to be worthy of Valhalla or the fields of Freyja, they recognized that they, like the gods they revered, were imperfect.

One of the chief ways that the Norse believed they could become worthy of life in Odin's Valhalla or

Freyja's Fólkvangr, was through courage in the face of an enemy, or kindness in the presence of a friend.

While much of the cycles of life and death have already been discussed, there is plenty more to know.

Now, we've established that Hel was the destination for most mortals, those who had brought dishonor upon themselves in one way or another; often through cowardice, treason or otherwise failing or harming their communities and each other.

The honored dead, however, had a much different future ahead of them. The honored dead who fell in battle were led by the Valkyries to Valhalla, or to Fólkvangr, where they would prepare, as their comrades under Odin's watch, for Ragnarök.

It's been stated that the honored dead would do battle in their preparation, and it's important to note that these battles weren't simple training exercises. Those doing battle were the Berserkers, warriors whose skill and fury in battle was unlike anything else on any of the worlds. Those who were bested in Valhalla were killed, just as if they were fighting a true war with one another. After the daily battle, those who had fallen would rise again, and all would come together to drink of mead and feast in each other's company.

Descriptions of Fólkvangr aren't as numerous or as detailed as those of Valhalla, but it's been postulated that the two destinations were of roughly the same nature. Freyja's half of the honored dead would also prepare for Ragnarök as an army; although, while Valhalla was generally the destination of men who had died on the battlefield, Fólkvangr also housed those of honor who were not warriors. Women, men and children could be found in Fólkvangr, but again, not much else is known about Freyja's army.

In their everyday life, the Norse held tightly to family bonds and the bonds with those of their communities with personal responsibility being at the forefront of their minds. This isn't to say that the Norse were a particularly peaceful people.

Vikings, as we know, were generally plunderers, at times conquering lands as far south as France and Spain. Those who stayed in their newly conquered lands, though, generally assimilated rather quickly into the general populous of their new surroundings.

Conquering or sacking the lands of foreigners was considered to be not only a way to prove one's honor and skill in battle, but as a way to strengthen and assert the Norse way of life. Though the Norse didn't believe in killing for the sake of killing, they did believe that if they killed or died in furtherance of strengthening their people, they would be greatly rewarded in the afterlife.

One of the chief reasons for this, and behind much of Norse morality, was how one's actions may influence Ragnarök. It could be said that while the honorable dead would strengthen the gods, therefore, perhaps, giving mankind and its deities a crucial edge in Ragnarök, cowards and criminals would do just as much damage as their cohorts did good.

Hel, despite its modern usage, was to the Norse, not a place of eternal damnation and punishment, but simply as a place where there really wasn't much going on. Furthermore, those who came to dwell in Hel would likely play a small roll (if any role at all) in the events of Ragnarök.

Social ties were viewed as crucial, as those who sought to individuate themselves from their tribes or communities would also end up on their own in the afterlife; specifically, a whole lot of time with Hel.

The concepts of Niflheim and Muspelheim were likely simple allegories to locations, though nonspecific, in nature. To the north of the Norse lands was coldness and barrenness attributed to Niflheim. To the south was the land of heat and fire, attributed to Muspelheim. Put simply, due to the Norse lands' location in the upper part of the northern hemisphere, (Norway, Finland, Denmark, Sweden, Iceland and Greenland,) the Vikings recognized that the more north they went, the colder the land was; the further south they went, the warmer.

The Norse, though devotees of their gods, believed just as strongly in the importance of family and societal ties; what every Viking desired from battle was either a valiant death, or a great victory in which their fellows would all reap the benefit.

CHAPTER 7

From Chosen Tradition to Conversion

This is a small chapter, but it's crucial in Norse history, as it spelled the end for much of the Vikings' ability to hold their chosen religious beliefs. In this chapter, it's not my aim to say that one or the other religion is right or wrong, as that's a personal decision, all for themselves and it's certainly not my place, my goal or my business what anyone else believes. It is, however, useful to give a history of what happened and how.

Early attempts by the Catholic Church (mainly in the eighth and ninth centuries) to convert those in modern-day Scandinavia were largely unsuccessful. Though a few baptisms were performed, and the Catholics did set up some churches, headed by representative leaders among the religion of the time, many among the Norse simply didn't want to give up their traditional beliefs.

In Denmark, where the Vikings were more commonly ruled by local chieftains than by farther reaching authorities, there was a particularly strong antipathy toward Christianity. While raiding in Christian lands, many, though not all, of the individual Viking tribes would bring back Christian slaves or, in some cases, wives—also, assumedly under similar duress as the slaves—as trophies of their conquest.

Those who did convert to Christianity early on often held their traditional beliefs as well, not wanting to offend their old gods and local spirits. The first major converts, such as the Danish King, Harald Klak, did so in order to win favor, and thus, support from the Christian armies or political arms.

Others converted through trickery, such as Harald "Bluetooth" (Blåtand) Gormsson. Gormsson, who, though he had remained pagan for much of his rule had allowed missionaries in his lands, finally converted after a monk held a hot piece of iron in his hand without sustaining injury. This move was also politically motivated, though, as he sought the support of the church's armies in defending his homeland from Germany.

In Norway, when early attempts at conversion failed, Harald Greyhide set about sacking Viking temples and holy sites. This, unsurprisingly, didn't go over too well with the Norse.

While the individual reasons for conversion varied, early on at least, very few are thought to have converted due to a change in faith. Those who were not in positions of political power often converted in order to obtain the fine gifts which the missionaries brought them or, in some cases, to escape the threat of death had they not converted. Even those of higher station in the Viking lands were enamored at the immense wealth of the church, sometimes converting to get a piece of the pie for themselves.

Over time, though, much of the formerly Norse lands converted to Christianity. Some peoples held out against the church, such as the people of Greenland and the Samis in Norway and Sweden who didn't convert en masse until the early 1800s.

Even after the conversion of large populations within the Scandinavian countries, though, many of the people continued to practice their Tradition, though they had to do so in secret.

In time, the formerly Norse lands would join the Christian ranks, even sending many of their warriors to participate in the Crusades. For a time, Christianity was the predominant religion claimed by the peoples of Scandinavia.

Fast-forward to the present day. While much of Scandinavia remains Christians, countries such as Sweden and Denmark have become increasingly secular, even to the point of being among the most secular societies in the world today. Some areas throughout the Scandinavian world hold a great amount of anger toward Christian establishments for what they view as the destruction of their original and chosen culture.

What the future may hold for Christianity in Scandinavia is uncertain and up for debate, but many of these formerly Viking peoples have returned to forms of their earlier beliefs.

CONCLUSION

Thanks again for reading this book!

We've travelled far and wide, uncovering some of the tales and triumphs of the Norse Tradition. While there will always be more to discover, I hope that you have found this text both informative and enjoyable.

If you would like to learn more about the Norse Tradition, I highly suggest picking up a copy of the Poetic Edda. It's the closest we have to a primary source on Norse mythology, written by the Norse themselves. The Prose Edda is also a valuable source. Although it may not have the same veracity as the Poetic Edda, it does have some valuable insight into this compelling Tradition of beliefs.

Although the worlds may have met their demise, just like the Norse Tradition itself, that is a long way from being the end of the story. Mythologies, like civilizations, may rise and fall, but what they leave behind tells us not only of a distant past populated with strange people whose beliefs differ from our own, but gives us all an insight into the world in which we live today. Although the Norse Tradition was almost exclusively practiced in Scandinavia, its residue can now be found worldwide, and its stories have inspired many modern tales of life and death, courage and disgrace.

So, whether you're reading this as an informational overview, or for entertainment, I hope that you've found something to strike your fancy and whet your appetite for history. I use the term history there purposefully, not to imply that these gods and myths were actual events, but in the way that these same influenced countless generations of Norse peoples and continues to do so today.

It has been my honor and privilege to bring you this brief glimpse into the fantastical world of Norse mythology, and I hope that you have enjoyed reading it. Check out the other books in this series, including: Discovering Ancient Egypt, Discovering Ancient Egyptian Mythology, Discovering Ancient Greece and Discovering Ancient Greek Mythology.

The ways of the Vikings will live on to inspire people the whole world over in stories, entertainment and academia. What I love most about history and the mythologies of different peoples is that, regardless how those societies and cultures may different from our own, wherever we may live, our truth and heritage can be found therein. The world over and throughout history, people are people. While we often differ in our belief systems, our politics or even our general approaches to life, there is a common thread throughout. We can always learn from the past and from each other, and I hope we do.

It has been an utter joy to share some of the fascinating world of the Norse with you. I wish you happy reading, and a continued thirst for history!

Thank you,

Martin R. Phillips

A Preview of
Martin R. Phillips'
Latest Book

EGYPTIAN MYTHOLOGY

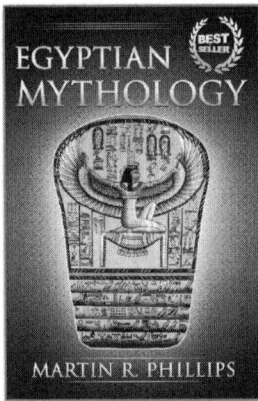

The mythology of ancient Egypt is a vast and fascinating thing to study. With up to seven-hundred gods and goddesses (and combinations thereof,) the mythology of the ancient Egyptians was complex and, like all religions thus far, would undergo changes in theory and practice over time.

There's something so compelling about the ancient Egyptians that their culture and beliefs are still popular today. Although most of the country no longer practices the religion of the ancients, figures such as Isis, Osiris, Horus and Set (to name a very few) still pop up in movies, music, art and philosophical discussion.

The mythology of the ancient Egyptians is now worldwide, and is without doubt, one of the most enduring and fascinating sets of mythos that the world has ever seen.

One of the most intriguing things about the Egyptian mythology is that there are actually a number of parallels between it and later mythologies, such as that of the Greeks, the Romans; even modern day Judaism, Christianity and Islam have many similarities with these ancient myths.

But there is that which sets the mythology of the ancient Egyptians apart. Somehow it's regal and elegant. Like many other mythologies, there are tales of good and evil, sex and violence, creation and destruction, love and loss. The phenomena of nature, humans, animals, emotions, life, love and death are contained within the vast and often inscrutable sources from which we have come to glean the meaning behind the glyphs and learn more about one of, if not the most, important cultures and mythologies the world has seen.

It's important to note that many of the Egyptian myths that we are aware of only began to be recorded during the old kingdom (approx. 2686-2181 B.C.) through use of what we now call The Pyramid Texts.

These were prayers, myths and incantations carved into the walls of the burial chambers of ancient Egypt's most important figures to ensure their safe passage to the afterlife.

The origins of Egyptian mythology are lost to antiquity; however, what we do know is more than enough to keep one busy studying for a lifetime. The pharaohs would come to be regarded as gods upon the earth, incontestable gateways between all of mankind and the realm of the gods; however, little mention of the pharaohs themselves will be made in this particular text. Here, we are primarily concerned with that which is outside the realm of governance; at least as far as it doesn't concern the religion of the ancient Egyptians.

In Egyptian mythology, we have the idea of the soul, of justice, balance, both on earth in life and after death in an afterlife... for a very short period, we even see a transition from paganism (belief in multiple gods) to monotheism (belief in one god,) although this change would not last.

The principles and morals of the ancient Egyptians are brought to life through their mythology. One of the easiest ways of understanding a people is to familiarize one's self with their beliefs, whether religious or secular, and I am very excited to take this journey with you into a realm of better understand-

ing one of the most enigmatic societies that the world
has ever known...

PS. If you enjoyed this book, please help me out by kindly leaving a review!

Martin R. Phillips

13235412R00050

Printed in Poland
by Amazon Fulfillment
Poland Sp. z o.o., Wrocław